Children's Illustrators

Ezra Jack Keats

Jill C. Wheeler
ABDO Publishing Company

visit us at
www.abdopub.com

Published by ABDO Publishing Company, 4940 Viking Drive, Edina, Minnesota 55435.

Printed in the United States.

Cover Photo: Kerlan Collection, University of Minnesota Libraries
Interior Photos: Corbis pp. 12, 13, 16, 20, 21; Ezra Jack Keats Foundation pp. 7, 9, 11, 15, 23; Kerlan Collection, University of Minnesota Libraries p. 5; Prospect Park Archives p. 19

Series Coordinator: Jennifer R. Krueger
Editors: Kate A. Conley, Stephanie Hedlund, Kristin Van Cleaf
Art Direction: Neil Klinepier

Special thanks to Dr. Deborah Pope for her help with this project.

Library of Congress Cataloging-in-Publication Data

Wheeler, Jill C., 1964-
    Ezra Jack Keats / Jill C. Wheeler.
        p. cm. -- (Children's illustrators)
    Includes bibliographical references and index.
    ISBN 1-59197-718-5
    1. Keats, Ezra Jack--Juvenile literature. 2. Illustrators--United States--Biography--Juvenile literature. I. Title.

NC975.5.K38W49 2004
741.6'42'092--dc22
                                                                    2004046107

Contents

The Art of Everyday

In the early 1930s, the United States was in the **Great Depression**. Thousands of people were jobless and had little money. Many struggled to find food and shelter.

Young Ezra Jack Keats saw the effects of the Depression every day. He lived in a poor part of New York City. He enjoyed climbing to the top of his family's apartment building to look out at the neighborhood.

Keats loved to paint what he saw every day from his rooftop. He painted **cityscapes** and people of all colors. In high school, he painted a picture of some homeless men huddled around a fire to stay warm. It was a sight Keats saw quite often in those days.

Keats entered the painting in a national contest. It won first place. Later, he worked on books for children and adults. In all, he wrote or illustrated more than 85 of them. Many were about things Keats saw in his own life. He made art from the everyday.

Opposite Page: *Ezra Jack Keats was one of the first children's book illustrators to include minorities living in big cities as major characters.*

Growing Up in Brooklyn

Ezra Jack Keats was born on March 11, 1916, in Brooklyn, New York. Ezra's parents were Benjamin and Augusta Katz. Both had **immigrated** to the United States from Poland. The couple hoped to escape **persecution** that Jews faced there. They also hoped to make a better life for their children.

Unfortunately, there was **discrimination** against Jews in America, too. When Ezra was born, his parents named him Jacob Ezra Katz. Ezra found it extremely difficult to get work as an artist when his name sounded Jewish.

Ezra put his middle name first and changed his last name. He found work more easily this way. Ezra remained proud of being Jewish for his whole life. With the name Keats, he was also able to earn his own living.

Ezra was the third child in his family. He had an older brother, Kelly, and an older sister, Mae. The family lived in a small apartment. Benjamin worked as a waiter at a coffee shop. Augusta stayed home with the children. They always worried about having enough money for food and rent.

Unfortunately, they had little money for special things, such as new clothes or books. Ezra owned only a handful of worn books, but he loved to read. So, he often borrowed books from libraries and friends. Ezra read every art book he could get his hands on.

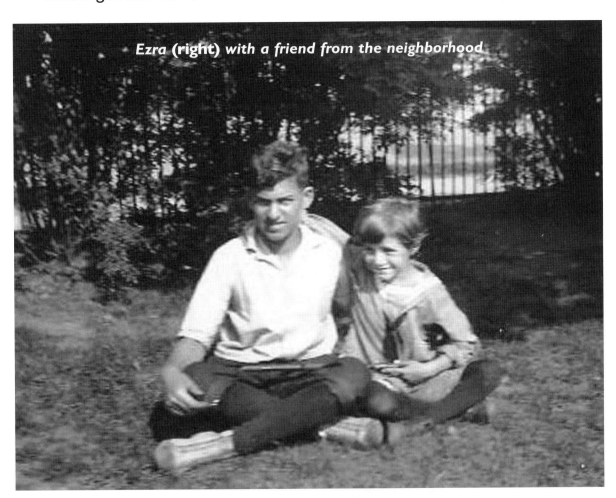

Ezra (right) with a friend from the neighborhood

Table Art

Ezra began showing artistic talent at an early age. As a child, he drew pictures on the family's kitchen table. They were pictures of small houses and people from many lands.

Augusta was not angry with her son for drawing on the table. Instead, she complimented him on his artwork. She proudly showed the drawings to visitors. Then, she covered them with a tablecloth to keep them safe.

Benjamin was proud of his son, too. Yet he worried about Ezra's future. Benjamin knew artists did not usually make much money. So, he warned Ezra not to dream of being an artist.

Ezra knew his father was worried. But, he could not bring himself to give up painting. Instead, he began to hide his work from his father.

Ezra and his mother worked to keep his painting a secret. Augusta allowed Ezra to paint after school. He would stop when he heard his father's footsteps on the stairs. Sometimes, Benjamin smelled the paint anyway. Then, he would order Ezra to go outside and play.

Drawing wasn't Ezra's only talent. He also played the ukulele, which is a small guitar.

Tough Neighborhood

Ezra was not always happy about going outside to play. He lived in a tough neighborhood. One day when Ezra was eight years old, a group of bullies stopped him. They began looking at the artwork he was carrying.

Ezra was ready for the worst. However, his paintings impressed the bullies. They soon began treating him better. He learned that art could make a difference, even in the worst neighborhoods.

Ezra's art opened another door shortly afterward. He earned a quarter for painting a sign for a local candy shop. Benjamin decided Ezra might be able to make a living painting signs.

Benjamin began bringing Ezra art supplies. He told his son he had gotten them at the coffee shop. He said some artists were so poor they traded art supplies for food. Later, Ezra realized his father was actually buying the supplies. He only told the stories to warn Ezra about living as an artist.

Ezra entered Thomas Jefferson High School in 1932. Just before his graduation, his father died of a heart attack. The police asked Ezra to look through Benjamin's wallet. Ezra was surprised to find clippings about art awards he had won. Ezra realized that his father was very proud of his talents after all.

By the time Ezra was a teenager, he knew that art was more than just a hobby for him. He dreamed of having a successful career even when his family had little money.

Making a Living

Keats had won several **scholarships** to art schools. However, he had no choice but to turn them down. He had to help take care of his mother now that Benjamin was gone.

The nation was still in the **Great Depression** when Keats graduated from high school. It was hard to find work as an artist. So, he took a job loading melons into a truck. He earned one dollar per day. He took night classes in art whenever he could afford to.

In 1937, Keats got a job painting **murals** for the Works Progress Administration (WPA). It was a government program that gave people jobs constructing public buildings, roads,

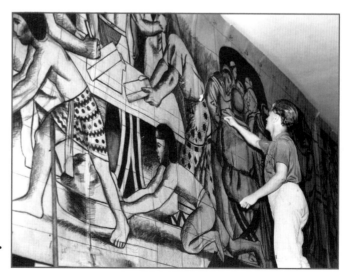

A muralist paints for the WPA.

and bridges. Keats worked for the WPA for three years.

After leaving the WPA, Keats became a comic book illustrator for Fawcett Publications. He was working on comics when the United States entered **World War II** in 1941.

Two years later, Keats decided to sign up for the United States Air Corps. It was part of the U.S. Army. He designed **camouflage** patterns and worked on training manuals.

Keats returned to his art when World War II ended in 1945. He spent nearly a year painting in Paris, France.

A Captain Marvel comic book. After several promotions, Keats was allowed to draw Captain Marvel's head!

These paintings were different from his previous work. His earlier paintings showed the dark side of life in Brooklyn. In Paris, he switched to brighter watercolors.

A New Career

Keats returned to New York City after his time in Paris. He was able to sell some of his work by displaying it in New York City storefronts. He also designed book covers.

He was then asked to illustrate a children's book called *Jubilant for Sure*. It was published in 1954 and was honored as one of the 50 best children's books of the year. This success led to more illustrating assignments. However, Keats wanted to make his own stories come to life.

In the late 1950s, Keats began working with a writer named Pat Cherr. They worked on a book called *My Dog Is Lost!*; *Mi Perro Se Ha Perdido*. It is about Juanito, an eight-year-old boy who loses his dog. Juanito speaks Spanish, so the story features both Spanish and English words.

The book was published in 1960 and quickly gained the attention of New York's Spanish-speaking community. Children were delighted to have a book that included Spanish words. They wrote Keats letters about how much they enjoyed the book.

These letters gave Keats more confidence to write his own stories. So, he began a new book. This time he would do both the writing and the illustrating. It would be his most successful effort yet.

Keats was delighted to read letters from children regarding **My Dog Is Lost.** *One read, "We would like to know about you. Are you Spanish? Do you have children? Do you make your own paint? My house paint is not such a real color. I would like the recipe for your paint."*

The Snowy Day

Keats began collecting materials for his new book. Most of the time, Keats painted his illustrations. Yet, he also enjoyed working with collages. Keats liked to pick materials that had interesting textures and colors. He also experimented with different ways to apply paint.

For some time, Keats had wanted to write a story about a boy he had seen in a 1940 issue of *Life* magazine. He decided to name the boy Peter. He made up a story about Peter's adventures on a snowy day in New York City.

Keats enjoyed making collages, which are pictures made from different materials with interesting textures and colors.

Keats titled his new book *The Snowy Day*. It was unlike any other children's book. It contained a mixture of texture and color. It also featured an African-American character. Few books at that time featured people of color.

The Snowy Day was published in 1962. Many readers said the book reminded them of what it was like to be a child. African-American children enjoyed seeing someone in a book who looked like them. *The Snowy Day* was awarded the **Caldecott Medal** in 1963.

Elements of Art

Texture

Texture is one of the most basic parts of art. Texture is how a piece of art feels or looks like it would feel. Keats used many tricks to create texture in *The Snowy Day*. For example, he used collage. In a collage, materials are glued onto a canvas. Keats used pieces of colored and textured paper in *The Snowy Day*.

He also used a special kind of paint with his collage work. He mixed watercolors with a kind of gum. It created a shiny surface on the canvas. Artists call this kind of painting *gouache*. This also added texture to *The Snowy Day*.

City Stories

The Snowy Day was the first of several books Keats wrote about Peter and his friends. All of them are stories about things children face every day.

In *Whistle for Willie*, Peter struggles to whistle for his dog. The book became very popular. In fact, a statue of Peter and Willie now stands in Prospect Park in Brooklyn.

Peter gets a new baby sister named Susie in *Peter's Chair*. A fourth story about Peter is *A Letter to Amy*. The story is about Peter's growing interest in girls. *Goggles!* is about how scary older kids can be to younger children. It was a runner-up for the **Caldecott Medal**.

Pet Show! is another book about Peter. It was published in 1972. Keats had now been writing about Peter for ten years. He felt Peter had grown up enough. He began writing stories about Peter's little sister, Susie.

Keats also wrote a series of stories about a character named Louie. Louie was one of Peter's friends. He lived in

Peter and Willie in Prospect Park

the city and was growing up without a father. Many children in single-parent families liked these books.

Parents and children were glad to see characters like Peter and Louie. The books were set in places where many children lived. Keats's characters played alongside the same traffic lights, tall buildings, and **graffiti** as his readers. This made Keats's books very popular.

Helping Children

Keats loved spending time with children. But, he never married or had children of his own. He just lived with his dog, Jake, and cat, Samantha. Keats loved helping young people whenever he could, however.

UNICEF was created in 1946.

Keats was able to help children around the world with a special project in 1966. He designed five greeting cards for the United Nations International Children's Emergency Fund (UNICEF). People bought more than 1 million of his cards.

Keats continued working into the 1980s. In 1983, he was illustrating a folktale called *The Giant Turnip*. He became ill that year with a heart problem. He even had surgery to correct the problem. However, it was not enough. Keats died of a heart attack on May 6, 1983. He was 67 years old.

Today, Keats's vision lives on through the Ezra Jack Keats Foundation. **Royalties** from Keats's books fund the foundation's programs. These programs help improve the lives of children through reading and art. Keats's books continue to entertain and teach children today.

The United Nations headquarters in New York City

Glossary

Caldecott Medal - an award the American Library Association gives to the artist who illustrated the year's best picture book. Runners-up are called Caldecott Honor Books.

camouflage - a pattern designed to blend into the surroundings for disguise.

cityscape - a view of a city.

discrimination - unfair treatment based on factors such as a person's race, religion, or gender.

graffiti - drawings on public buildings, sidewalks, and other structures.

Great Depression - a period (from 1929 to 1942) of worldwide economic trouble when there was little buying or selling, and many people could not find work.

immigration - entry into another country to live. A person who immigrates is called an immigrant.

mural - a picture painted on a wall or ceiling.

persecute - to harass someone because of his or her origin, religion, or other beliefs.

royalty - part of the money from the sale of a work that goes to the creator, such as an author or musician.

scholarship - a gift of money to help a student pay for instruction.

World War II - from 1939 to 1945, fought in Europe, Asia, and Africa. Great Britain, France, the United States, the Soviet Union, and their allies were on one side. Germany, Italy, Japan, and their allies were on the other side.

Web Sites

To learn more about Ezra Jack Keats, visit ABDO Publishing Company on the World Wide Web at **www.abdopub.com**. Web sites about Ezra Jack Keats are featured on our Book Links page. These links are routinely monitored and updated to provide the most current information available.

Index